# Preschool Art

# Painting

**MaryAnn F. Kohl**
**Illustrations: Katheryn Davis**

## Dedication

Dedicated in memory of my grandmother, Mary Geanne Faubion Wilson,
the first published author I ever knew, who sparked my imagination
when she told me that angels made my freckles
when they kissed me on the nose as I slept.

## Acknowledgments

I would like to thank my editor, Kathy Charner, for her humor and kindness
in our editor-author relationship. Sometimes I think we have too much fun to call this work!
In addition, I would like to thank the owners of Gryphon House, Leah and Larry Rood,
for their support and friendship, and their belief in this book and in me.
Most important, my thanks go to my husband, Michael,
and my daughters, Hannah and Megan, who keep my mind clear,
tell me when I've been wonderful or when I haven't and
remind me of what is most important in life.

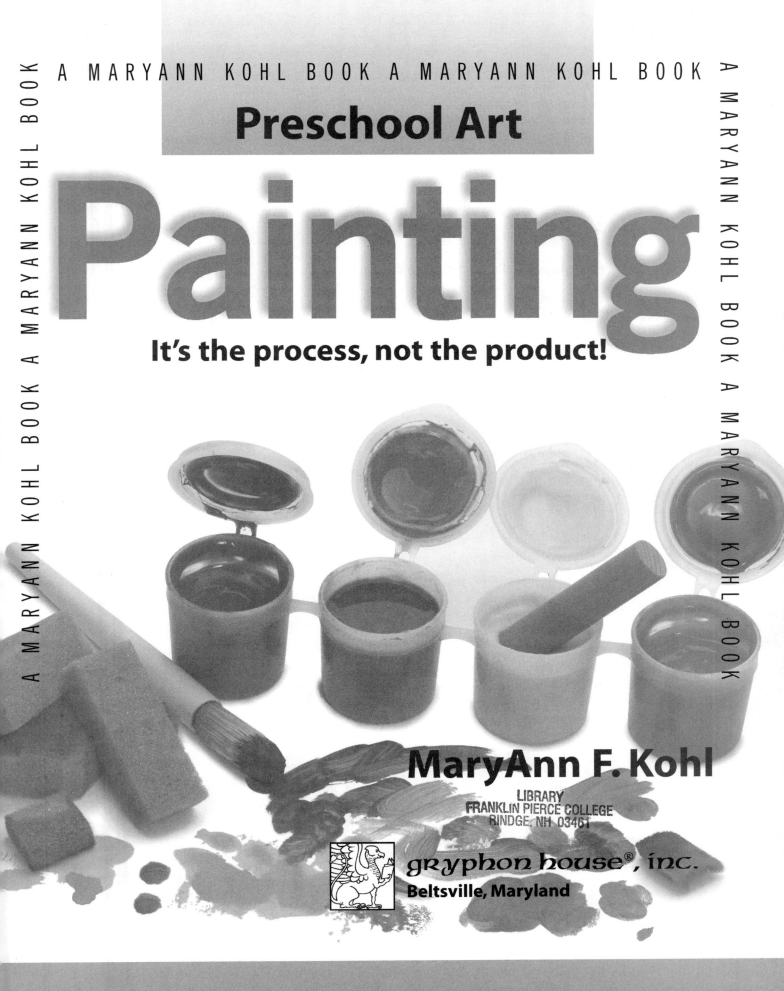

## Preschool Art

# Painting

### It's the process, not the product!

## MaryAnn F. Kohl

gryphon house®, inc.
Beltsville, Maryland

Text illustrations: Katheryn Davis

Library of Congress Cataloging-in-Publication Data

Kohl, MaryAnn F.,
    Preschool art: it's the process, not the product! / MaryAnn F. Kohl; [illustrations, Katheryn Davis].
        p.   cm.
    "A MaryAnn Kohl book."
    Inludes indexes.
    Contents: [1] Craft and construction --[2] Clay, dough, and sculpture -- [3] collage and paper -- [4] Painting -- [5] Drawing.
    ISBN 0-87659-224-8 (v.4)
    1. Art--Study and teaching (Preschool)--Handbooks, manuals, etc. I. Title: craft and construction. II. Title: Clay, dough, and sculpture. III. Title: Collage and paper. IV. Title: Painting. V. Title: Drawing. VI. Davis, Katheryn. VII. Title.
LB1140.5.A7 K64 2001
372.5'044--dc21

                                                                              2001018468

Illustrations: Katheryn Davis
Cover photograph: Rosanna, please fill in this information

## Bulk purchase

Gryphon House books are available at special discount when purchased in bulk for special premiums and sales promotions as well as for fund-raising use. Special editions or book excerpts also can be created to specification. For details, contact the Director of Marketing at the address above.

## Disclaimer

The publisher and the author cannot be held responsible for injury, mishap, or damages incurred during the use of or because of the activities in this book. The author recommends appropriate and reasonable supervision at all times based on the age and capability of each child.

# Table of Contents

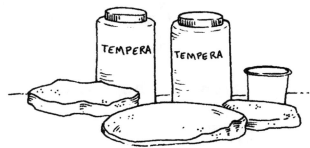

**Introduction** . . . . . . . . . . . . . . . . . . . .6

**Activities**

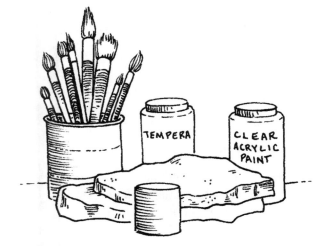

# It's the Process, Not the Product

## Why is art process important?

Young children do art for the experience, the exploration, and the experimentation. In the "process" of doing art, they discover creativity, mystery, joy, and frustration, which are all important pieces in the puzzle of learning. Whatever the resulting masterpiece—be it a bright sticky glob or a gallery-worthy piece—it is only a result to the young child, not the reason for doing the art in the first place.

Art process allows children to explore, discover, and manipulate their worlds. Sometimes the process is sensory, such as feeling slippery cool paint on bare fingers. Other times it is the mystery of colors blending unexpectedly, or the surprise of seeing a realistic picture evolve from a random blob of paint. Art process can be a way to "get the wiggles out," or to smash a ball of clay instead of another child.

## How can adults encourage the process of art?

Provide interesting materials. Stand back and watch. Offer help with unruly materials, but keep hands off children's work as much as possible. It's a good idea not to make samples for children to copy because this limits their possibilities.

Sometimes adults unknowingly communicate to a child that the product is the most important aspect of the child's art experience. The following comments and questions serve as examples of things to say that will help encourage each child to evaluate his or her own artwork:

| | |
|---|---|
| *Tell me about your artwork.* | *How did the paint feel?* |
| *What part did you like the best?* | *The yellow is so bright next to the purple!* |
| *I see you've used many colors!* | *How did you make such a big design?* |
| *Did you enjoy making this?* | *I see you made your own brown color. How did you do it?* |

Process art is a wonder to behold. Watch the children discover their unique capabilities and the joy of creating. This is where they begin to feel good about art and to believe that mistakes can be a stepping stone instead of a roadblock—in art as well as in other aspects of their lives. A concept children enjoy hearing is, "There's no right way, there's no wrong way, there's just your way."

# Getting Ready!

*Being prepared makes art experiences all the more enjoyable.*
*Here are some tips for success:*

## Covered Workspace

Cover the workspace—whether it is a table, floor, chair, wall, or countertop—with newspaper. Tape it down to prevent wiggles and spills of art materials. It's so much easier to bunch up sheets of paint-filled, sticky newspaper and find a clean space underneath than to clean up uncovered workspaces time and again. Other workspace coverings that work well are sheets of cardboard, an old shower curtain, a plastic table-cloth, big butcher paper, and roll ends of newsprint from the local newspaper print shop.

## Handy Cleanup

Make cleanup easy and independent for young artists. All the less worry for the adult in charge! Place a wet sponge or pads of damp paper towels next to the art project for a simple way to wipe fingers as needed. Rather than have children running to the sink, fill a bucket with warm soapy water and place it next to the work area. Then add a few old towels for drying hands. Damp rags and sponges are handy for wiping spills, tidying up, and cleaning splatters as needed.

## The Cover-up

An old apron, Dad's old shirt (sleeves cut off), a smock, and a paint shirt are all helpful cover-ups for creative preschoolers. Instead, consider this: wear old play clothes and old shoes and call them "art clothes," used for art only. It's a wonderful feeling to get into art without being concerned about protecting clothing. These clothes become more unique with time and are often a source of pride!

## Other Tips

- Create a separate drying area covered with newspapers. Allow wet projects to dry completely.
- Always protect a larger circle of space than the immediate area around the project. Think about floors, walls, and carpets (maybe even ceilings!).
- Shallow containers are often mentioned in the Materials lists. These include cookie sheets, flat baking pans, clean kitty litter trays, plastic cafeteria trays, painter's pans, and flat dishes and plates.
- It's never too late to start collecting recyclables for art. Save collage materials, fabric and paper scraps, Styrofoam grocery trays, yarn, sewing trims, and even junk mail.
- Wash hands thoroughly before starting any edible activity.
- Do activities inside or out unless specifically noted as an outdoor activity only.

# Using the Icons

Each page has icons that help make the projects in Painting more useable and accessible. The icons are suggestions only. Experiment with the materials, vary the suggested techniques, and modify the projects to suit the needs and abilities of each child.

## Age
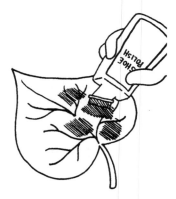
The age icon indicates the general age range of when a child can create and explore independently without much adult assistance. The "& Up" means that older children will enjoy the project, and that younger children might need more assistance. Children do not always fit the standard developmental expectations of a particular age, so decide which projects suit individual children and their abilities and needs.

## Planning and Preparation

The plan and prep icon indicates the degree of planning or preparation time an adult will need to collect materials, set up the activity, and supervise the activity. Icons shown indicate planning that is easy or short, medium or moderate, or long and more involved.

## Help

The help icon indicates the child may need extra assistance with certain steps during the activity from an adult or even from another child.

## Caution

The caution icon appears for activities requiring materials that may be sharp, hot, or electrical in nature. These activities require extra supervision and care.

## Hints
Hints are suggestions for the adults working with the artists.

# Easel Painting

## Materials

paint easel with clips
large sheets of newsprint or butcher
   paper
tempera paint
cups
large paintbrushes

## Art Process

1. Clip a small stack of
   paper to the easel. (Slip
   out the top sheet when a
   painting is complete; the next
   piece of paper will be ready for
   painting.)
2. Fill the cups with tempera paints mixed to
   a medium consistency to avoid runny drips. Use cups with snap-on lids
   that have a hole for the paintbrush (found in school supply stores). Empty
   yogurt cups and small milk cartons also work well.
3. Dip brushes into the paint and paint on the paper (see hints).
4. When the painting is complete, remove it from the easel and clip it to a
   drying rack.

## Variation

• Use other art materials such as chalk, watercolors, markers, or unusual paint
   recipes such as Vegetable Dye Paint (see page 13).

## Hints

• Young artists do not have the adult concept of keeping brushes in only one
   color of paint or keeping cups of paint clean. As much as adults would like
   the cups of paint to stay clean and unmixed with other colors, it may not
   happen.
• A fish net on the wall with clothespins provides a good drying area.

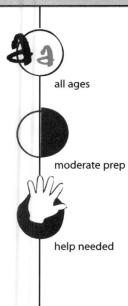

all ages

moderate prep

help needed

# Fingerpainting

## Materials
newspaper
large paper
liquid starch
powdered or liquid tempera paint

## Art Process

1. Place a piece of paper on a pad of newspapers.
2. Pour a puddle of liquid starch about the size of a slice of bread in the middle of the piece of paper.
3. Squeeze a blob of liquid tempera paint or a rounded spoonful of powdered tempera paint in the middle of the starch puddle.
4. Use fingers to smear and mix the paint.
5. After spreading the paint across the paper, begin to fingerpaint by moving fingers and hands through the paint. Elbows and arms make interesting designs, too!
6. If paint dries out, add a bit more liquid starch to the paper.
7. Carefully peel the finished project from the newspaper before it is completely dry to prevent the painting from sticking to the newspaper.

## Hints

- Glossy or shiny paper works best.
- This is a messy project. Even artists who cover their clothing still seem to get paint on their clothes.

# Watercolor Paint

## Materials
paintbrush
cup of water
watercolor paint
  box
paper

## Art Process
1. Dip a paint-brush in the cup of water and then into one of the watercolor paints.
2. Paint on the paper.
3. Rinse the brush and continue painting with the watercolor paints.
4. Change the rinse water when it gets murky.
5. Paint until the artwork is complete.

## Variations
- Experiment mixing colors in the lid of the paint box or on the paper.
- Paint on wet paper.
- Outline paintings with permanent marker after they have dried.

## Hint
- Young artists often hold up their paintings for adults to admire. Watercolor paintings are usually dripping wet, which can be a bit messy. Remind artists to hold their wet creations "flat" or to ask the adult to come to their work areas to view the creation.

# Runnies

## Materials
paper
cookie sheet
tape
tempera paint
cups
spoons

## Art Process
1. Place a piece of paper on a cookie sheet. Tape the corners to hold the paper in place.
2. Fill the cups with several colors of tempera paint mixed to a thin consistency and place a spoon in each cup.
3. Spoon one color of paint on the paper. Make paint tracks by tipping the cookie sheet, letting the paint run across the paper.
4. Now add another color. Tilt or tip the cookie sheet again. The colors will run into each other and mix together.
5. Add many colors and tip as many times as desired.
6. When finished, remove the paper from the cookie sheet and place in a drying area. Or, let the painting dry on the cookie sheet and remove later.

## Variations
- Place a puddle of paint on the paper and blow the paint in different directions using a drinking straw. Remind the artist to blow out so that no paint will be accidentally swallowed!
- Thick paint runs too, but may need a little coaxing with a paintbrush or toothpick to get it started.

## Hint
- The cookie sheet helps control spills and drips. It works best if it has sides.

# Vegetable Dye Paint

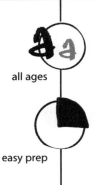

all ages

easy prep

## Materials
powdered vegetable food dye*
water
measuring spoons
mixing cup
liquid starch
stirring spoon

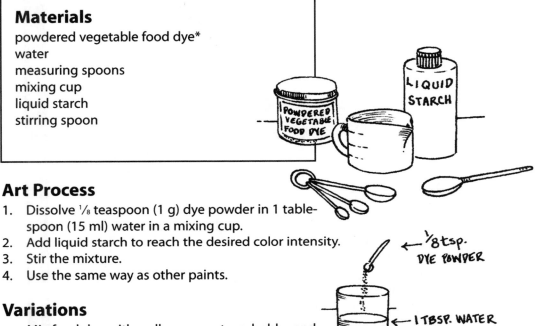

## Art Process
1. Dissolve ⅛ teaspoon (1 g) dye powder in 1 table-spoon (15 ml) water in a mixing cup.
2. Add liquid starch to reach the desired color intensity.
3. Stir the mixture.
4. Use the same way as other paints.

← ⅛ tsp. DYE POWDER

← 1 TBSP. WATER

## Variations
- Mix food dye with wallpaper paste or hobby and craft paste to make brilliant and translucent paint.
- Substitute food coloring for vegetable food dye.

ADD LIQUID STARCH...

## Hints
- * Powdered vegetable food dye is a harmless food coloring. This material makes the best paint the author has ever used.
- Powdered vegetable food dye is available at school supply stores in bright blue, dull blue, red, yellow, and green. The powders can be mixed to make new colors such as purple, brown, or orange.
- Paint made from food dye is somewhat transparent.

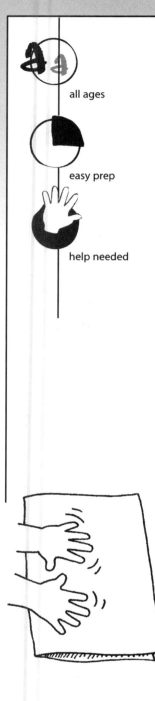

all ages

easy prep

help needed

# Paint Blots

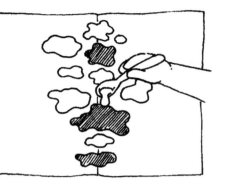

**Materials**
tempera paint
cups
paper, pre-folded
   down the middle
spoons or
   paintbrushes
scissors, optional

## Art Process
1.  Fill the cups with tempera paints.
2.  Open the pre-folded piece of paper and place it on the work surface.
3.  Use a spoon or paintbrush to drop blobs of paint on the fold or on one side of the paper.
4.  Fold the paper and gently rub or press the two sides of the paper together. Press out from the fold toward the edges of the paper.
5.  Unfold the paper to see what the "blot" looks like.
6.  Continue making more blots on new paper. Think about what shapes might occur and what colors might mix together well.
7.  After the picture has dried, use scissors to cut out the design if desired.

## Variation
•   Cut out blots into butterflies, flowers, bugs, or other imaginary things; for the more advanced artistic thinker, attempt to make shapes such as a heart, snowflake, pumpkin, or other form.

## Hint
•   Pressing gently seems to be an important factor in controlling blots. To test the technique, make a blot by pressing really hard. Next, make another blot by pressing gently.

# Monoprint

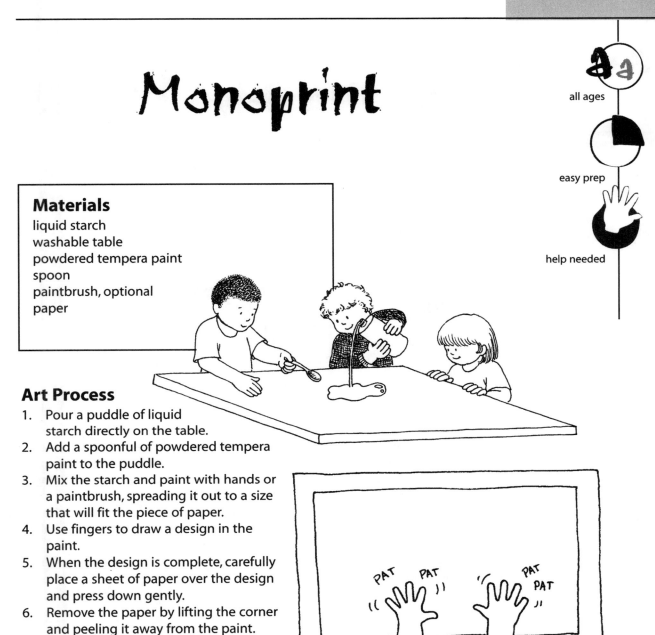

## Materials
liquid starch
washable table
powdered tempera paint
spoon
paintbrush, optional
paper

## Art Process
1. Pour a puddle of liquid starch directly on the table.
2. Add a spoonful of powdered tempera paint to the puddle.
3. Mix the starch and paint with hands or a paintbrush, spreading it out to a size that will fit the piece of paper.
4. Use fingers to draw a design in the paint.
5. When the design is complete, carefully place a sheet of paper over the design and press down gently.
6. Remove the paper by lifting the corner and peeling it away from the paint.
7. A monoprint of the design will appear on the paper.
8. Make additional prints using the same design or make a new design.

PAT PAT PAT PAT

## Variations
- Add more than one color of paint to the puddle of starch and experiment with mixing colors.
- Instead of painting on the table top, paint on a sheet of Plexiglas or on a cookie sheet.

## Hints
- If the paint on the table dries out, add more starch.
- To flatten curled, dry paintings, iron them (adult only).

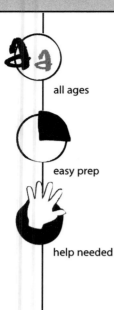

all ages

easy prep

help needed

# Dip and Dye Papers

<table>
<tr><td>

**Materials**
sheets of newsprint
food coloring or powdered dye
water
cups
coffee filters, paper towels, napkins,
   or white tissue paper
eyedroppers
iron, optional

</td></tr>
</table>

## Art Process

1. Place a sheet of newsprint on the work surface.
2. Put food coloring or powdered dye mixed with water into cups.
3. There are several techniques you can use in Dip and Dye. The easiest one is to place a paper towel (or other type of paper) on the sheet of newsprint and use an eyedropper to squeeze drops of food coloring or dye onto the paper towel.
4. Another technique is to fold the paper towel and dip its corners into the cups of dye. Carefully unfold the paper towel and place it on the sheet of newsprint.
5. When dyeing a thin paper such as white tissue, unfold the wet, dyed paper as far as possible without tearing and allow it to dry overnight. Finish unfolding the dry paper the next day. When the paper is completely dry, iron it if necessary (adult only).

## Hints

- Paper dyes are highly concentrated powder dyes and can be purchased at art stores. Although fairly expensive, the powdered dyes will last for years and the colors are incredibly bright and vibrant. In the long run, they are cheaper and better than food coloring (see page 13).

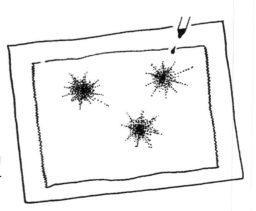

- Experiment with dipping and dying any of the papers suggested. A coffee filter works best when folding and dipping in cups of dye.

# Paint and Print

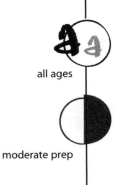

all ages

moderate prep

## Materials
paper towels
pan or tray
liquid tempera paint
things to make prints (see list)
paper

## Art Process
1. Place a stack of wet paper towels in a pan or tray.
2. Spread liquid tempera paint on the paper towels to make a print pad.
3. Press an object (see list) onto the print pad and then press it onto a piece of paper. Press the object onto the paper several times. To make more prints, press the object onto the print pad again.

## Variations
- Experiment using ink, food coloring, watercolor paints, thick and thin tempera paints, or paper and fabric dye.
- Make wrapping paper, a wall hanging, greeting cards, or a framed poster.
- Wrap string around a block of wood or an empty toilet paper roll to make a string print.

### Things to Make Prints
fingertips
gadgets
inflated balloons
kitchen utensils
sponges
toys

## Hint
- Encourage young artists to press gently onto the print pad and onto the paper. Some young minds think that the harder and louder they whack the object into the paint and then onto the paper, the more impressive the print will be.

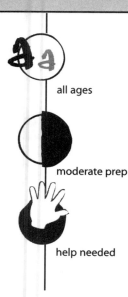

all ages

moderate prep

help needed

# Handy Prints (Footie, Too)

## Art Process

1. Pour several colors of thick tempera paints into separate trays. Using three different colors works well.
2. Use a paintbrush to paint your hand or press your hand into the paint.
3. Press the painted hand onto the paper.
4. Repaint the hand with a new color or the same color. Continue printing on the paper. Try overlapping colors to make new colors.
5. Wash and dry hands with the soapy water before carrying the print to a drying area.
6. Make footprints too! Follow the same procedure using feet instead of hands. Walk on a piece of long paper or make single prints on small paper.

## Variations

- Make a single handprint on a paper plate.
- Make prints using other parts of the body such as the nose or elbow. Be creative!

## Hint

- A hand washing bucket or a large, shallow tub usually works better than a sink. A bucket is easy to clean and easy to use. Change the water in the bucket as often as needed. The paint usually stains the skin but wears off in a day or two.

# Powder Paint

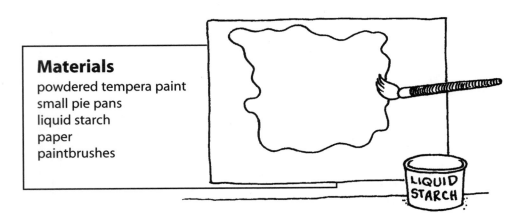

## Materials
powdered tempera paint
small pie pans
liquid starch
paper
paintbrushes

## Art Process
1. Place powdered tempera paint into small pie pans.
2. Pour a puddle of liquid starch on a piece of paper.
3. Use a paintbrush to spread the starch on the paper.
4. Dip a clean, slightly damp paintbrush into the powdered paint and dab it onto the starch-covered paper.
5. The paint will dissolve and become thicker, creating an unusual texture.

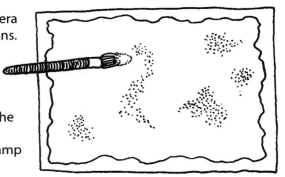

## Hints
- Big heavy paper, such as butcher paper, works well.
- Pie pans can flip over. Use flat Styrofoam grocery trays taped to the table when working with younger children.

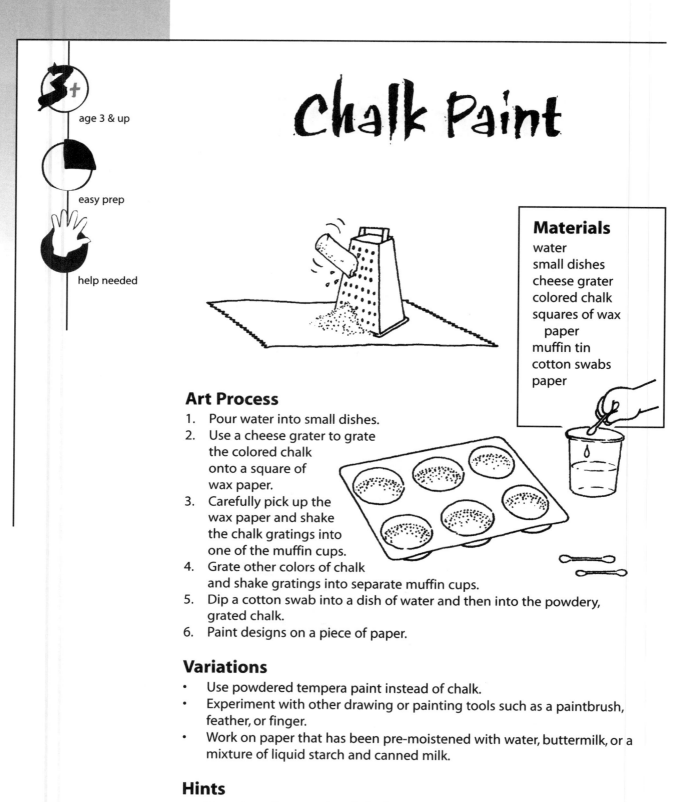

age 3 & up

easy prep

help needed

# chalk Paint

## Materials
water
small dishes
cheese grater
colored chalk
squares of wax
    paper
muffin tin
cotton swabs
paper

## Art Process
1. Pour water into small dishes.
2. Use a cheese grater to grate
   the colored chalk
   onto a square of
   wax paper.
3. Carefully pick up the
   wax paper and shake
   the chalk gratings into
   one of the muffin cups.
4. Grate other colors of chalk
   and shake gratings into separate muffin cups.
5. Dip a cotton swab into a dish of water and then into the powdery,
   grated chalk.
6. Paint designs on a piece of paper.

## Variations
- Use powdered tempera paint instead of chalk.
- Experiment with other drawing or painting tools such as a paintbrush,
  feather, or finger.
- Work on paper that has been pre-moistened with water, buttermilk, or a
  mixture of liquid starch and canned milk.

## Hints
- To make a fine powdered chalk, crush the chalk with a hammer or rock
  instead of using a cheese grater.
- Art chalk works better than the dustless chalkboard variety.

# Mystery Paint

## Materials

baking soda
water
tablespoon
cup
cotton swabs
white paper
paintbrush
watercolor paint

## Art Process

1. Dissolve 4 tablespoons (60 g) baking soda and 4 tablespoons (60 ml) water in a cup.
2. Dip a cotton swab into the mixture and paint an invisible picture on the white paper.
3. Allow the artwork to dry completely.
4. Dip a paintbrush into the watercolor paint and brush paint over the invisible picture to reveal the "mystery picture."

## Variations

- Create a secret picture or message for a friend to reveal using watercolor paint.
- Draw an invisible picture using a white crayon and then brush with watercolor paint to create a mystery wax resist.

## Hint

- Very young artists can be skeptical about painting something they can't see, but they will soon catch on to the fun.

age 3 & up

moderate prep

# shiny Paint

## Materials

small containers
liquid tempera
 paint
corn syrup
liquid dishwashing
 soap
measuring spoons
mixing spoons
paintbrushes
matte board or
 cardboard

## Art Process

1. In small containers, mix each color of liquid tempera paint with 4 tablespoons (60 ml) corn syrup and 1 ½ teaspoons (7 ml) dishwashing soap.
2. Dip a paintbrush into mixture and paint freely on matte board or cardboard, which provide a sturdy base.

## Variations

- Place paper on a baking pan and pour small puddles of Shiny Paint onto it. Then roll marbles through the puddles.
- Use the Shiny Paint on white or colored tissue paper to create wrapping paper.

## Hints

- This paint is very pretty and glossy, which makes it nice for holidays.
- This paint is also very sticky and dries more slowly than regular paint.

← 1 ½ TBSP. DISHWASHING SOAP

4 TBSP CORN SYRUP

STIR!

# Glossy Paint

### Materials

white drawing paper
scissors
4 colors of food coloring
sweetened condensed milk
4 cups
paintbrushes or cotton swabs
bulletin board
pushpins

## Art Process

1. Cut shapes from the white drawing paper or draw shapes on the paper.
2. Mix a different color of food coloring with condensed milk in each of the four cups.
3. Use a paintbrush or cotton swab to paint the shapes with the different colors.
4. While the paint is still wet, use pushpins to hang the shapes on a wall, letting the paint colors run together. (A fence or bulletin board work, too.)
5. Allow the art to dry for several days.

## Variations

- Use this paint idea for painting or designing eggs for Easter or spring themes.
- Mix a combination of bright colors and pastel colors.

## Hints

- Young children may need help carrying the painted shape, using pushpins, and keeping control of the project.
- Cover the floor beneath the dripping paint.

age 3 & up

3+

age 3 & up

moderate prep

help needed

# Roller Fence Painting

## Art Process

1. Tape a large sheet of butcher paper to an outdoor fence.
2. Fill the trays with different colors of tempera paint.
3. Roll the paint rollers in the trays of paint.
4. Paint on the butcher paper using the paint roller.

## Hints

- Do not do this project on the ground or artists may end up crawling through the paint.
- The textures of the fence materials, such as wire or wood, will appear on the painting.
- Keep clean-up materials handy!

## Materials

masking tape
large butcher paper
outdoor fence
large trays
tempera paint
paint rollers,
   different types
   and sizes
bucket of soapy
   water and rags

# Fence Mural

age 3 & up

moderate prep

help needed

## Materials

tape or stapler
roll of wide, heavy
  paper
long fence
tempera paint
cans or wide bowls
paintbrushes
small tables, chairs,
  or boxes,
  optional

## Art Process

1. Tape or staple a long, wide, heavy roll of paper securely to a fence. (Use lots of tape or staples so the paper will not tear and fall down.)
2. Pour the tempera paint into cans or wide bowls.
3. Place the containers of paints and brushes at intervals along the fence.
4. Several artists can paint at the same time on the same long piece of paper.

## Variations

- Act out a play and use the mural as a backdrop or for scenery. Layer several murals so they can be easily changed for different scenes.
- Agree on a theme and paint a scene with a group of artists. Some suggestions are Houses in Our Neighborhood, Dinosaur World, Wild and Big Colors, Around the World, Summer Fun, or The World's Biggest Painting.

## Hints

- Small tables, flat chairs, or strong cardboard boxes work well as paint stands.
- Scraps of heavy paper are often available free from newspaper printers. These are often the ends of heavy paper rolls.
- Fence murals make great party activities.
- To reduce the amount of dripping, mix paints fairly thick and add liquid starch for smoothness.

# Rock Painting

## Materials

flat rocks, any size
tempera paints
cups
medium-point
    paintbrushes
clear acrylic craft
    paint, optional

## Art Process

1. Collect flat rocks at the beach, along a river, or purchase them from a landscape garden supplier.
2. Place rocks on the work surface.
3. Pour tempera paint into cups.
4. Dip a medium-point brush into the paint and paint a design on the rock.
5. If painting the underside of the rock too, let the top dry before turning the rock over. When dry, turn the rock over and paint the underside of the rock.
6. If desired, cover the design with clear acrylic craft paint to protect it.

## Variations

- When the basic design on the rock is dry, use a fine-point brush to add details.
- Use markers to make the design or to add details to a dry, painted rock.
- Use the finished product for paperweights, bookends, or table decorations.
- Stack and glue rocks together to make painted rock sculptures.

## Hint

- Older children can use acrylic paints, which won't wash or smudge off the rock when dry.

# Foil Painting

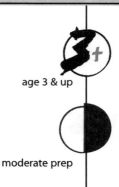

age 3 & up

moderate prep

---

## Materials

matte board or cardboard
aluminum foil
tape, optional
measuring cup
thick tempera paint
cup
measuring spoons
dishwashing liquid
paintbrushes

---

## Art Process

1. Cover a piece of matte board or cardboard with aluminum foil, folding the foil around the back of the board.
2. Tape the foil, if desired.
3. Pour ½ cup (115 ml) thick tempera paint in a cup.
4. Add 1 teaspoon (5 ml) dishwashing liquid to the tempera paint.
5. Paint on the foil.

## Variation

- Cover a box, bottle, or picture frame with foil.

## Hint

- The dishwashing liquid helps the paint adhere to foil, plastic, or other glossy surfaces. If the paint isn't sticking, add another ½ teaspoon (2 ml) of dishwashing liquid to the paint.

BACK OF
CARDBOARD

# Twist and Shout

## Art Process

1. Put a large scrap of laminate from a counter top on the floor.
2. Fill squeeze bottles with tempera paint.
3. Squeeze 3 to 4 big drops of paint directly on the scrap of laminate.
4. Place a piece of heavy paper on the drops of paint.
5. Use the heel of the palm to twist the paper about half a turn.
6. Lift the paper to see the design.
7. Continue to experiment using different colors and types of twisting to create new designs.
8. Sponge off the laminate with soapy water to make way for new creations or a change of artists.

## Materials

large scrap of laminate from a counter top
squeeze bottles
tempera paints
heavy paper
sponge and soapy water

## Variations

- Make twisting designs using bare feet, with or without paper.
- Use other types of paper to make the twisting design.
- Use a table or a cookie sheet instead of a scrap of laminate.

## Hint

- Wash off the laminate between artists or when a new creation is started. This project works well outdoors where a bucket or hose can be used to clean the laminate easily.

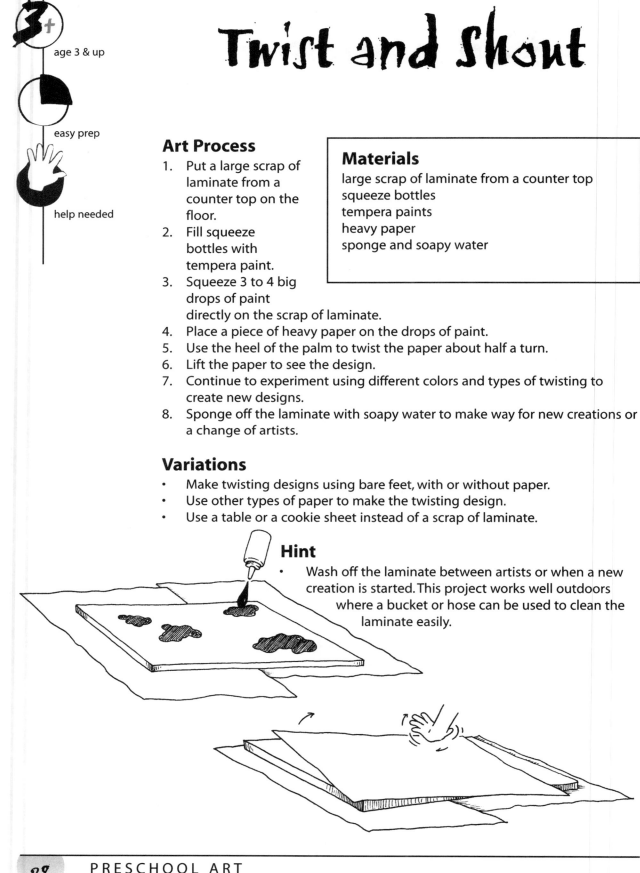

# Salad Spinner

## Materials

scissors
paper
plastic salad spinner
liquid tempera paints
cups
spoons
glitter or confetti, optional

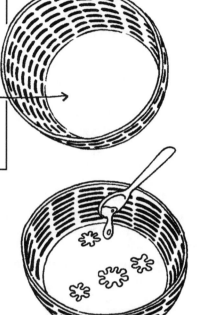

PLACE PAPER
IN BOTTOM...

## Art Process

1. Cut paper to fit into the bottom of the salad spinner.
2. Place the paper in the spinner.
3. Pour tempera paint into cups.
4. Dip a spoon into a cup of paint and drip paint onto the paper. Use more than one color, if desired.
5. Snap the lid onto the spinner and use the handle to spin it.
6. Take off the lid and add glitter or confetti, as desired.

## Variation

- Think of other spinning ideas, such as an old record player or a lazy Susan. Experiment with paint, markers, and crayons.

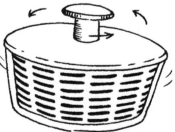

age 3 & up

moderate prep

# Tissue Stain

## Art Process

1. Tear tissue paper into small pieces.
2. Place torn bits of tissue paper on the matte board or white cardboard. Use one color or several colors.
3. Fill the spray bottles and a cup with water.
4. Spray water on the tissue pieces. Dip a paintbrush into the cup of water and paint over the tissue pieces. This will enhance the staining from the tissues.
5. Peel away the wet tissue pieces from the cardboard and a stained design will remain.
6. After the design has dried, add more colors if desired.

### Materials
tissue paper, 3 or 4 colors
matte board or white cardboard
water
spray bottles
cup
paintbrushes

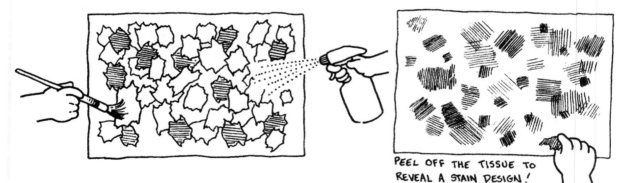

PEEL OFF THE TISSUE TO REVEAL A STAIN DESIGN!

## Variations
- Experiment using hard-boiled eggs, white fabric, paper towels, coffee filters, napkins, or white tissue paper instead of cardboard.
- Cut the cardboard or matte board into a holiday or theme shape, such as a heart for Valentine's Day.

## Hint
- Fingers will become stained, so keep a bucket of soapy warm water and a towel handy. Sometimes it takes several days for the stain to wear off.

# Paper Drop Dye

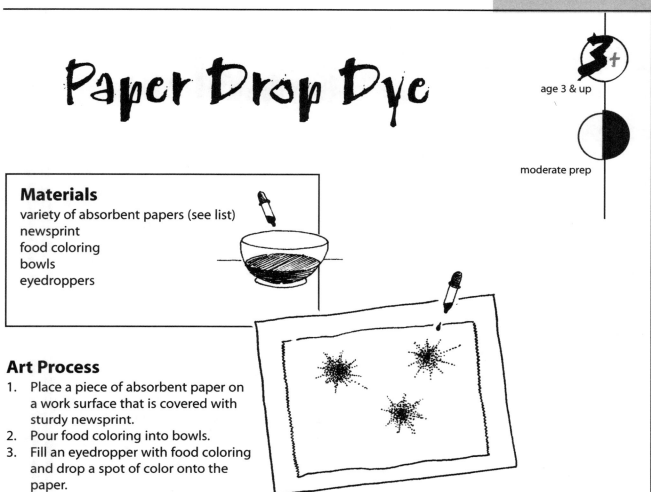

## Materials
variety of absorbent papers (see list)
newsprint
food coloring
bowls
eyedroppers

## Art Process
1. Place a piece of absorbent paper on a work surface that is covered with sturdy newsprint.
2. Pour food coloring into bowls.
3. Fill an eyedropper with food coloring and drop a spot of color onto the paper.
4. Use another eyedropper to add a different color. The colors will blend and make a pattern.
5. Transfer the paper to a clean piece of newsprint to dry.

## Variation
• When the project is dry, cut the paper into a design such as a snowflake, use it as wrapping paper, or hang it in a window.

## Hints
• Many young artists become absorbed with the blending of colors and end up with a soaked piece of paper, which can be difficult to move. Work on a sheet of newsprint that is sturdy enough to hold the finished artwork and can be lifted and carried to a drying location.
• Expect fingers and hands to become stained; the color can take several days to wash off.

### *Types of Absorbent Papers*
rice paper
coffee filter
blotting paper
paper towels

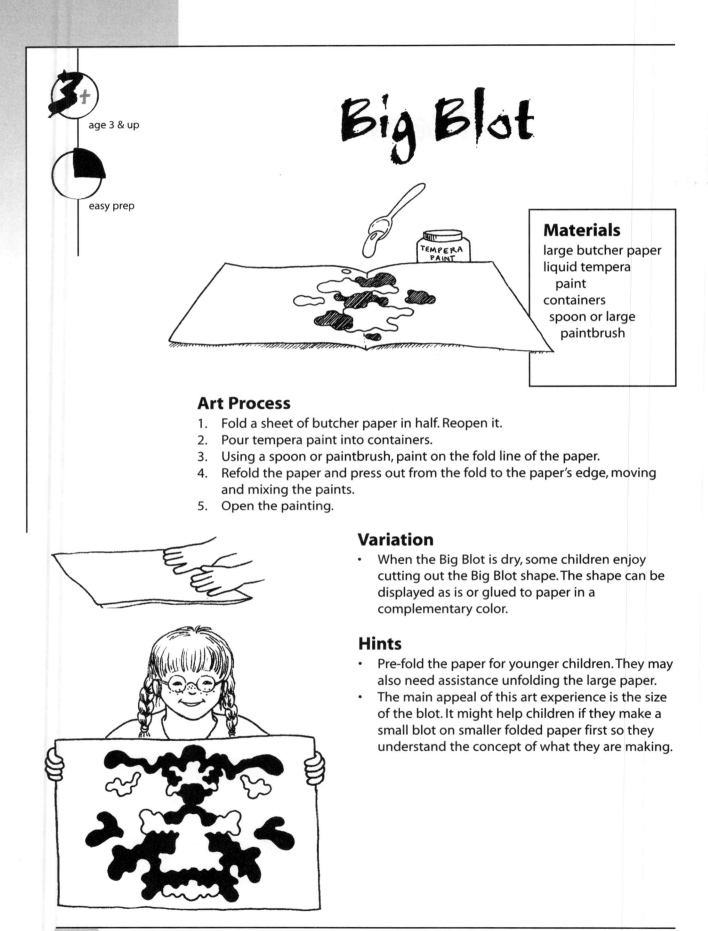

# Big Blot

## Materials
large butcher paper
liquid tempera
   paint
containers
 spoon or large
   paintbrush

## Art Process
1.   Fold a sheet of butcher paper in half. Reopen it.
2.   Pour tempera paint into containers.
3.   Using a spoon or paintbrush, paint on the fold line of the paper.
4.   Refold the paper and press out from the fold to the paper's edge, moving and mixing the paints.
5.   Open the painting.

## Variation
•   When the Big Blot is dry, some children enjoy cutting out the Big Blot shape. The shape can be displayed as is or glued to paper in a complementary color.

## Hints
•   Pre-fold the paper for younger children. They may also need assistance unfolding the large paper.
•   The main appeal of this art experience is the size of the blot. It might help children if they make a small blot on smaller folded paper first so they understand the concept of what they are making.

# Corncob Print

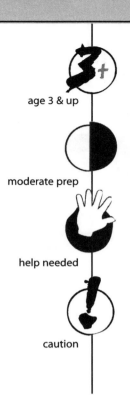

age 3 & up

moderate prep

help needed

caution

## Materials

tempera paint
cookie sheet or tray
corn holders or
 nails
dried corncobs
large paper

## Art Process

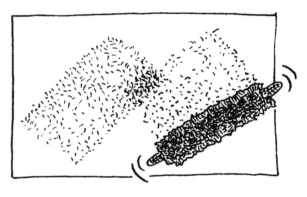

1. Pour puddles of tempera paint on a cookie sheet or tray.
2. Push corn holders into the ends of the corncob to use as handles while painting. If holders are not available, push nails into each end of the cob. Supervise closely.
3. Roll the corncob through the paint on the cookie sheet (like a paint roller).
4. Take the paint-covered cob and roll it across the large sheet of paper. Roll one long line or use back-and-forth movements. Make designs or shapes.

## Variation

- Use the corncob print for gift wrap or as backgrounds for other projects.

## Hints

- Save corncobs after the corn has been eaten and dry them on a shelf.
- Sometimes this project works best on the floor so active artists can really roll the corn.
- Corncobs can be reused by rinsing them in water and letting them dry.

# Fingerpaint Leaves

**Materials**
big autumn leaves
newspaper
fingerpaint
containers
bucket of soapy
    water and towel
big paper or
    newsprint

## Art Process

1. Collect big autumn leaves (such as maple leaves) that are still fresh.
2. Place a leaf on a piece of newspaper.
3. Pour fingerpaint into containers.
4. Dip fingers in the fingerpaint and smooth and smear paint all over one side of the leaf.
5. Use fingers to draw designs into the paint on the leaf.
6. Wash and dry hands.
7. Place a sheet of newsprint or paper over the leaf and gently pat the paper onto the painted leaf.
8. Carefully peel the paper from the leaf or peel off the leaf from the paper.
9. An imprint from the fingerpainting and the leaf will be transferred to the paper.

## Variation

- Place leaves under the paper and rub the paper with peeled crayons to create leaf rubbings.

## Hint

- A simple fingerpaint recipe is to mix ¼ cup (60 ml) liquid starch and 1 tablespoon (15 ml) powdered or liquid tempera paint and stir it together. Try experimenting with different measurements to change the color, intensity, and thickness of the paint.

# Fingerpaint Mono-Stencil

## Materials

scrap construction
  paper
scissors
masking tape
large paper
liquid starch
cookie sheet
tempera paint
spoon
liquid detergent,
  if necessary
newspaper
bucket of soapy
  water and towel

## Art Process

1. Cut out a shape such as a circle, a leaf, or another object from construction paper.
2. Cut off a piece of masking tape, roll it into a small loop, and place it on the back of the shape.
3. Tape the shape to the center of a sheet of large paper.
4. Pour a puddle of liquid starch in the middle of the cookie sheet. Place a spoonful of powdered or liquid tempera paint in the starch puddle.
5. Use fingers to mix the starch and paint; continue fingerpainting on the cookie sheet. (If the paint is "resisting," add a few drops of liquid detergent to the fingerpaint.)
6. When the design is complete, place the paper with the shape (shape side down) over the cookie sheet. Gently press and pat the paper onto the fingerpainting design to make a monoprint.
7. Carefully peel the paper from the cookie sheet and place it on a piece of newspaper to dry.
8. After it has dried, gently peel or pull the paper shape from the painting.

## Hint

• The drying area should be next to the printing area.

LOOP OF TAPE ON BACK!

REMOVE THE SHAPE!

moderate prep

help needed

# Snow Paint

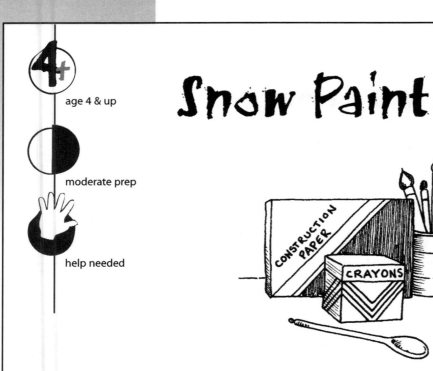

## Materials

measuring cups
  and spoons
hot water
Epsom salt
small cup or bowl
mixing spoon
crayons
dark construction
  paper
paintbrushes

## Art Process

1. Mix ¼ cup (60 ml) hot water with 4 tablespoons (80 g) Epsom salt in a small cup or bowl. Stir the mixture until the salt dissolves.
2. Use crayons (purple or blue work well) to draw on the dark construction paper.
3. Dip the paintbrush into the salt mixture and brush the drawing.
4. After the painting has dried, the salt will leave a snowy, crystal-like effect.

## Variation

• Cut out designs, such as snowflakes, from the paper and hang them by a string.

## Hints

• Stir the salt water often to keep the brush full of very salty water.
• When the picture is dry, the salt crystals brush off the paper.
• Substitute table salt or rock salt for Epsom salt.

ADD 4 TBSPS. EPSOM SALTS
AND STIR!

# Cornstarch Paint

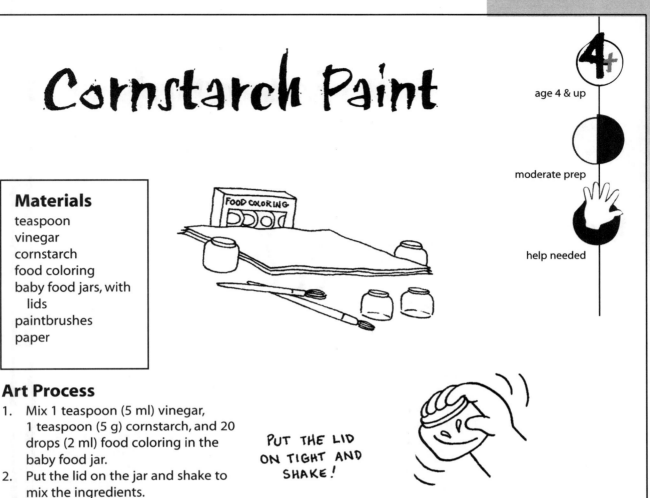

## Materials

teaspoon
vinegar
cornstarch
food coloring
baby food jars, with
    lids
paintbrushes
paper

## Art Process

1. Mix 1 teaspoon (5 ml) vinegar, 1 teaspoon (5 g) cornstarch, and 20 drops (2 ml) food coloring in the baby food jar.
2. Put the lid on the jar and shake to mix the ingredients.
3. Make several different colors in separate jars.
4. Dip a paintbrush into the cornstarch paint and paint on a piece of paper.

PUT THE LID ON TIGHT AND SHAKE!

## Variation

• Experiment using the paint on other surfaces, such as hard-boiled eggs.

## Hints

• Double or triple this recipe to make a large supply of paint.
• Substitute cream or paste food coloring (found in cake-decorating departments) to make brighter paints.
• Food coloring can stain clothing, so have soapy water and towels handy. Cover children and table surfaces to prevent spills from staining.

# Egg Paint

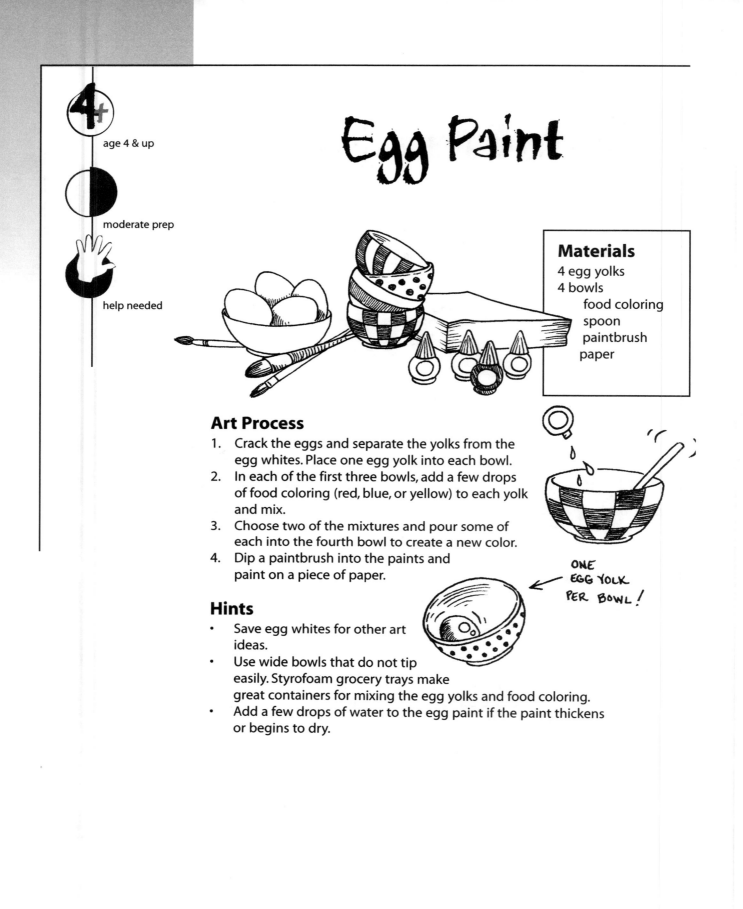

## Materials
4 egg yolks
4 bowls
    food coloring
    spoon
    paintbrush
    paper

## Art Process
1.  Crack the eggs and separate the yolks from the egg whites. Place one egg yolk into each bowl.
2.  In each of the first three bowls, add a few drops of food coloring (red, blue, or yellow) to each yolk and mix.
3.  Choose two of the mixtures and pour some of each into the fourth bowl to create a new color.
4.  Dip a paintbrush into the paints and paint on a piece of paper.

## Hints
*   Save egg whites for other art ideas.
*   Use wide bowls that do not tip easily. Styrofoam grocery trays make great containers for mixing the egg yolks and food coloring.
*   Add a few drops of water to the egg paint if the paint thickens or begins to dry.

ONE EGG YOLK PER BOWL!

# Spray Painting

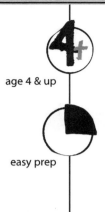
## Materials
heavy white paper
tempera paints
cups
paintbrushes
spray bottle
water

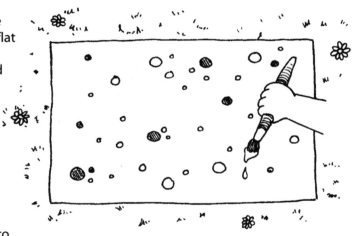

CLEAR WATER

## Art Process
1. Place the heavy white paper outdoors on a flat surface, such as grass, or inside on a covered floor.
2. Mix tempera paint to a medium consistency and pour into the cups.
3. Use a paintbrush to drip paint onto the paper.
4. Fill the spray bottles with water. Set them to spray, not stream.
5. Spray water on the drops of paint. The paint drops will thin, spread, and mix together.

## Variations
- Sprinkle dry tempera paint on heavy butcher paper and spray it with water.
- Try doing this project on a rainy day. Carry it outside and let the rain moisten it.
- Hang the paper on a fence so that the paint runs down. Allow the project to dry on the fence before removing it.

## Hint
- This is a good outdoor project because it allows plenty of room for spraying.

# Sprinkle Paint

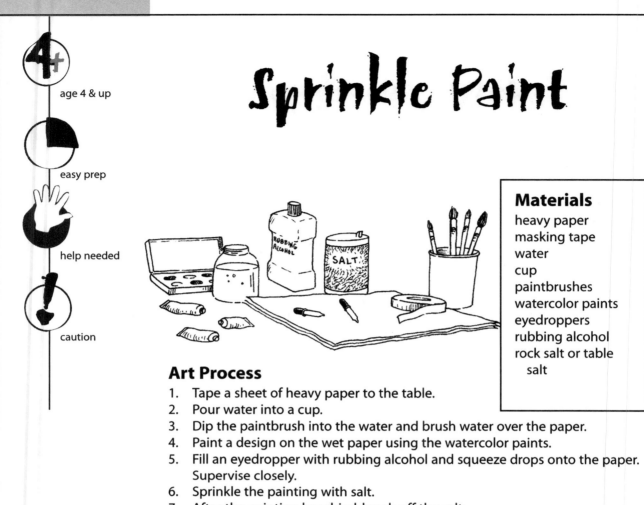

## Materials
heavy paper
masking tape
water
cup
paintbrushes
watercolor paints
eyedroppers
rubbing alcohol
rock salt or table
  salt

## Art Process
1.  Tape a sheet of heavy paper to the table.
2.  Pour water into a cup.
3.  Dip the paintbrush into the water and brush water over the paper.
4.  Paint a design on the wet paper using the watercolor paints.
5.  Fill an eyedropper with rubbing alcohol and squeeze drops onto the paper.
    Supervise closely.
6.  Sprinkle the painting with salt.
7.  After the painting has dried, brush off the salt.

## Hints
*   The rubbing alcohol and salt create an unusual artistic effect. However, you
    may prefer to skip step 5 and sprinkle the painting with salt without using
    alcohol.
*   Use big brushes that hold a lot of water.
*   Allow the painting to dry on the table rather than moving it to another area.

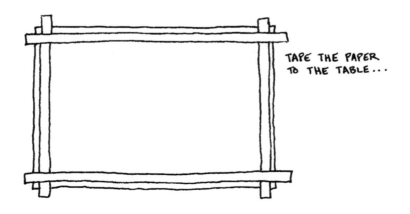

TAPE THE PAPER
TO THE TABLE...

# Stained Glass Painting

age 4 & up

easy prep

## Materials

plastic or newsprint
white drawing paper
non-toxic permanent black marker
bright liquid tempera paint
cups
paintbrushes

## Art Process

1. Cover the table with plastic or newsprint.
2. Use the permanent marker to draw bold, black lines on the drawing paper.
3. Pour the tempera paint into the cups.
4. Paint inside the black lines.

## Variations

- Use shiny paint instead of tempera paint. (See Shiny Paint on page 22.)
- Paint the black lines using black tempera paint. Wait for the lines to dry before painting inside of them.

## Hints

- Permanent markers soak through the paper and can stain the table, so cover the table with plastic or newsprint. If any marks get on the table, use powdered cleanser to remove them.
- To remove pen marks from clothing, spray the stain with hair spray, rinse, and repeat. Continue doing this until the stain is completely gone.

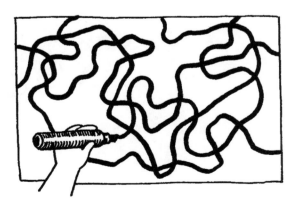

# Flicker Paint

## Art Process

1. Soak the sponge in water.
2. Use the sponge to wet both sides of a sheet of drawing paper.
3. Dip a paintbrush into the watercolor paint and drip drops of it onto the paper. Try flicking or shaking the paint on the paper, too.
4. Continue flicking, shaking, or dripping other colors onto the paper. The colors will blend and mix on the wet paper.
5. Allow the paintings to dry in place rather than moving them.

## Hint

• This is a good outdoor project because flicking the paint may spot inside walls. Put the paper on the grass and place rocks on it to keep it in place.

### Materials

sponge
water
white drawing
   paper
paintbrushes
watercolor paint

SOAK BOTH SIDES!

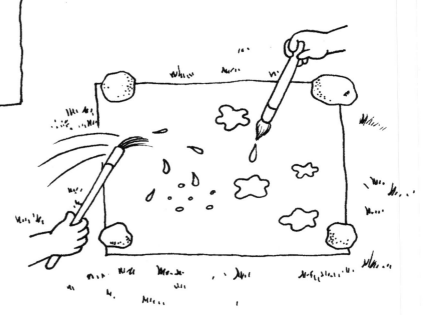

# Swinging Paint

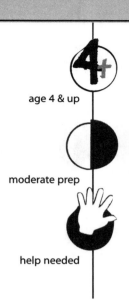

## Materials

plastic or newsprint
masking tape
large paper
string
scissors
paintbrushes, in a variety of sizes
tempera paint
trays or cans

## Art Process

1. Cover the floor with plastic or newsprint.
2. Tape a large sheet of paper to the covered floor.
3. Cut pieces of string and tie them to the handles of a variety of paintbrushes.
4. Pour the tempera paint into separate trays or cans.
5. Dip a paintbrush into the paint.
6. Stand over the sheet of paper and hold the paintbrush by the string so that it touches the paper.
7. Swing the paintbrush against the paper.
8. Refill the paintbrushes with paint, as needed.

## Variation

- Hang other objects from strings such as a cotton swab, a pencil, nuts, bolts, or an eraser. Dip these items in the paint and make designs on the paper.

age 4 & up

involved prep

help needed

# Easy Pendulum Paint

## Art Process

1. Tie a piece of string around the large opening of a plastic funnel.
2. Cut three pieces of string about 15" (37 cm) long. Tie or tape each string at equal intervals around the large edge of the funnel.
3. Tie the three ends together above the funnel.
4. Mix the liquid starch and powdered tempera paint in the small pitcher. Mix it to a consistency that will allow it to flow smoothly, but is not too thin.
5. Hold the pendulum funnel and string over the paper. With your other hand, place your finger over the spout of the funnel.
6. Pour the paint into the funnel. When the funnel is full, remove your finger and give the funnel a swing.
7. Swing the pendulum funnel until all the paint has run out of it.
8. Add a new color to the funnel and continue painting, if desired.

### Materials

strong string
small plastic funnel
scissors
tape
liquid starch
powdered tempera paint
small pitcher
large paper

## Variations

- Balance a dowel between two chairs and hang the pendulum funnel from it. Proceed by adding paint and removing your finger from the spout to release the paint.
- Use colored or plain sand or salt and dry tempera paint mixed together instead of paint. Proceed as above.

## Hint

- This project takes some coordination and timing, but it is great fun and allows artists to create very interesting designs.

# Shoe Polish Leaves

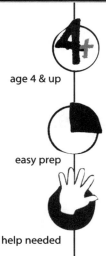

## Materials
fresh autumn leaves
newsprint
shoe polish in applicator
    bottles
variety of papers

## Art Process
1. Collect fresh autumn leaves in a variety of shapes and sizes.
2. Place a leaf on a piece of newsprint, face-side down.
3. Dab shoe polish over the back surface of the leaf.
4. Select a piece of paper and place it over the shoe-polished leaf. Gently press and pat the paper over the leaf.
5. Peel the paper from the leaf to reveal the leaf print.

## Variations
- Place a leaf on a sheet of paper. Dab shoe polish around the outside edges of the leaf, brushing out from the edges and onto the paper. Remove the leaf to reveal a stencil design.
- Experiment by using other leaves, changing polish colors, and using different types of paper.

## Hints
- Shoe polish stains hands and fingernails. Keep clean-up materials nearby.
- Shoe polish leaf prints show the veins and features of leaves in detail.

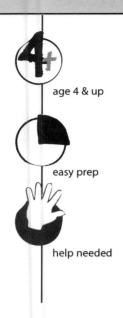

age 4 & up

easy prep

help needed

# Sponge Wrap

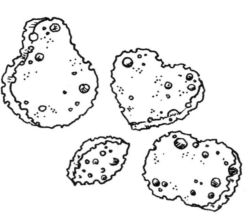

## Art Process

1. Cut sponges into shapes, such as leaves, fruits, hearts, or pumpkins.
2. Mix water and paste food coloring in a Styrofoam grocery tray.
3. Open a sheet of white tissue paper and place it on the work surface.
4. Dip a sponge into the color mixture and then press it onto the tissue paper. The sponge tends to stick to the paper, so carefully pull apart the sponge and paper.
5. Dip other sponges into the color mixture and continue printing on the paper.
6. Allow the tissue paper to dry completely. Fold and save the paper or use it immediately for wrapping paper.

## Variation

- Make prints using other items, such as cork, parts of toys, blocks, or cookie cutters.

## Hints

- Keep a paintbrush handy to dab extra coloring onto the sponges.
- If wrapping paper later gets wet, the design can rub off onto clothing or hands. For "stain-proof" coloring, use fabric or paper dye. It is slightly expensive, but it goes farther, comes in a larger variety of colors, and lasts longer than paste food coloring.

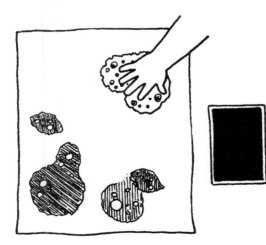

# Rolling Pattern

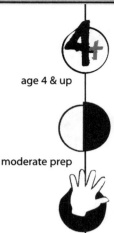

## Materials
fresh leaves
cardboard
white glue
spoon
tempera paint
cookie sheet
brayer*, print roller, child's rolling
  pin, or dowel
absorbent paper

## Art Process
1. Arrange the leaves into a design on the cardboard.
2. Glue the leaves to the cardboard and allow the glue to dry.
3. Place a spoonful of paint on the cookie sheet. Roll the print roller or brayer through the paint until it is evenly coated.
4. Roll the paint-covered roller over the leaves.
5. Place a piece of the absorbent paper on top of the leaves.
6. Rub the paper with clean, dry hands.
7. Peel off the paper and the raised veins and edges of the leaves will be imprinted on the paper.

## Variations
• Try using the same technique with wire mesh, lace, or netting instead of leaves.
• Mix different colors of paint on the cookie sheet to create a swirl of colors on the leaves.

## Hints
• Moist, fresh leaves work best for this project.
• * Brayers are art rollers that are available at art supply and school supply stores.

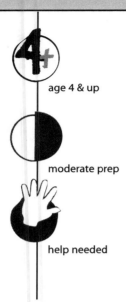

age 4 & up

moderate prep

help needed

# Insoles Stamps

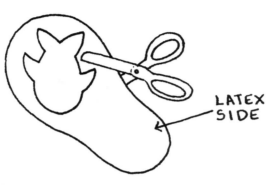

LATEX SIDE

## Materials
shoe insoles
pen
scissors
rubber cement
scrap of wood
 block
ink pad or paint,
 paper towels, and
 Styrofoam tray
paper or tissue
 paper

## Art Process
1. Use a pen to draw a design on the latex side (not the fabric side) of the insole.
2. Cut out the design.
3. Glue the shape to the scrap of wood using rubber cement.
4. When the rubber cement has dried, press the block stamp into an ink pad. Use a commercial ink pad or make your own by placing a pad of paper towels into a Styrofoam tray and spreading paint or food coloring over it.
5. Press the stamp onto a piece of paper or tissue paper.

## Variations
• Glue an insole shape to the top of a jar lid or a piece of heavy cardboard.
• Use this idea to decorate holiday wrapping paper or to make greeting cards.

## Hints
• Young children may think that the harder they smash the stamp into the ink, the better the print will be. Encourage them to apply firm but gentle pressure to make the best print.
• If you prefer not to use rubber cement (it has a strong odor) or if it is not available, you may substitute other glues.

RUBBER CEMENT

# Five Block Prints

## Materials

printing materials (see list)
scissors
5 wooden blocks
white glue
old washcloth
water
cookie sheet
tempera paint
paper

## Art Process

1. Cut each of the five printing materials (see list) into shapes or patterns and glue each one to a block of wood. (The insulation tape will stick without glue.)
2. Allow the glue to dry.
3. Dampen an old washcloth with water and wring it out.
4. Place the damp washcloth on the cookie sheet.
5. Spread tempera paint on the washcloth to make a stamp pad.
6. Press one of the block stamps into the stamp pad and then onto a piece of paper.
7. Continue printing on the piece of paper using one or several blocks.

## Variations

- Use food coloring, paste food coloring, dye, inks, or ink pads instead of paint.
- Make wrapping paper by printing on large sheets of white tissue.

### Printing Materials

insulation tape, peel-off variety
Styrofoam tray
scraps of felt
strips of cardboard
string

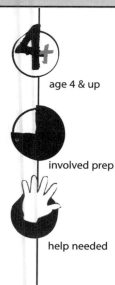

age 4 & up

involved prep

help needed

# Stamp-a-Doodle

HARDENED PLASTER

← CLAY

TEAR AWAY STYROFOAM...

## Materials

scissors
Styrofoam cup
play clay or
   plasticine
printing materials
   (see list)
plaster of Paris
paper towel
Styrofoam tray
tempera paint
paintbrush or
   spoon
paper

## Art Process

1.  Cut the Styrofoam cup in half. Discard the top half of the cup.
2.  Press some of the clay into the bottom of the cup.
3.  Make indentations in the clay using the various printing materials and then remove the items.
4.  Mix the plaster of Paris to a creamy consistency.
5.  Pour the plaster of Paris into the cup until it is about 1" (2 cm) deep.
6.  When the plaster has hardened and dried, remove it from the cup along with the clay. The plaster section is the stamp.
7.  Fold a paper towel into thirds and place it in a Styrofoam tray. Pour tempera paint on the paper towel.
8.  Spread the paint with a paintbrush or a spoon.
9.  Press the stamp into the paint and then press it onto a piece of paper.

## Hints

*   Plaster hardens quickly, so have everything ready when it's time to pour.
*   Although this project is fairly involved, it is worth the time and trouble because of the interesting stamps children can create.

### Printing Materials

beads
buttons
corks
small objects
small tiles

AFTER YOU PEEL THE CLAY, YOU HAVE A HARDENED PLASTER STAMP!

# Bubble Prints

## Materials

tempera paint
liquid detergent
measuring cup
quart container
water
stirring stick or
   spoon
shallow cake pan
straws (not flexible)
paper

## Art Process

1. The night before the project, mix $1/3$ cup (80 ml) tempera paint with $1/3$ cup (80 ml) liquid detergent in a quart container.
2. Add water to fill the container and stir the solution. Make separate quart solutions for each color of paint.
3. Allow the paint mixture to sit overnight.
4. The next day, pour the paint mixture into a shallow cake pan.
5. Using the straw, gently blow into the mixture to form bubbles.
6. Gently press a piece of paper onto the bubbles. The bubbles will pop and leave a print on the paper.

## Variation

• Blow bubbles into a pan containing detergent and water only. When the bubbles are thick and high, add a few drops of food coloring to the bubbles. Press a piece of paper or a paper plate onto the bubbles to make a print.

## Hints

• Cut a little nick or hole near the blowing end of the straw to prevent children from sucking the soapy solution into their mouths.
• To make strong bubbles that last, add a few tablespoons of sugar to the quart solution.

age 5 & up

moderate prep

help needed

# Chalky Leaf Spatter

## Art Process

1. Cut out one side of a cardboard box.
2. Place a sheet of paper inside the box and tape the edges down.
3. Place leaves, flowers, grass, or paper shapes on the paper.
4. Staple a wire screen to an old picture frame.
5. Place the framed wire screen several inches above the paper.
6. Mix the tempera paint to a thin consistency and pour it into a bowl.
7. Dip the nail brush into the paint. Rub the paint-filled brush across the screen many times. If you saturate the brush with paint, the spatter drops will be bigger and coarser.
8. Take a piece of chalk and rub it across the screen. Bits of chalk will fall through the screen and land in the wet paint, adding additional color to the spatter design. If the screen is clogged with paint, rinse it, shake it dry, and then add the chalk.
9. Allow the artwork to dry. Then remove the leaves and other objects.

## Hint

- The box will control the splattering paint. However, it can be messy, so make sure the artist wears an old shirt or art clothes.

| Materials |
|---|
| scissors |
| large cardboard box |
| paper |
| tape |
| pressed leaves, flowers, grass, or paper shapes |
| stapler |
| wire screen |
| old picture frame |
| tempera paint |
| bowl |
| nail brush |
| chalk |
| old shirt |

# Print Relief

age 5 & up

moderate prep

help needed

## Materials

newspaper
pen
squares of cardboard
scissors
glue
liquid tempera paint
shallow pan
paintbrush
paper or cloth
brayer, print roller,
    child's rolling pin, or
        dowel

## Art Process

1.  Cover the table with newspaper.
2.  Draw a design on a cardboard square.
3.  Cut out the design from the cardboard.
4.  Glue the design onto another piece of cardboard. Place it on the newspaper, design-side up.
5.  Pour tempera paint into a shallow pan.
6.  Paint the cardboard design.
7.  Place a piece of cloth or paper over the design.
8.  Roll the brayer or rolling pin over the cloth or paper to make a print.
9.  Peel the cloth or paper away from the cardboard to reveal the print.

## Variation

• Brush different colors onto different parts of the design to make a multi-colored print.

## Hints

• Young artists have a very hard time cutting cardboard; offer help as needed.
• Sometimes the paper folds over and sticks to itself when you peel it from the design. To prevent it from folding, peel it off using both of your hands.

age 5 & up

moderate prep

help needed

# Marbling

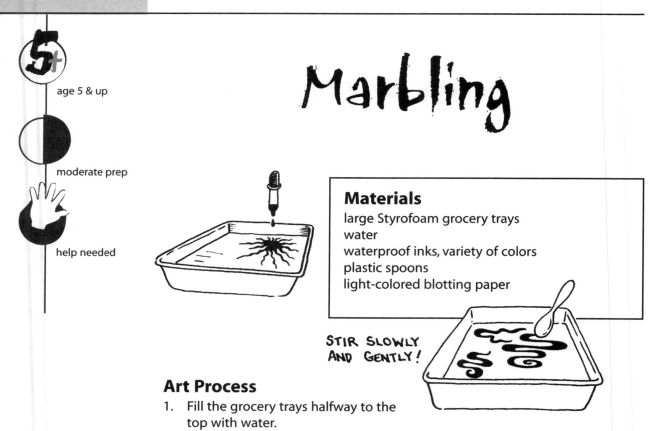

### Materials
large Styrofoam grocery trays
water
waterproof inks, variety of colors
plastic spoons
light-colored blotting paper

STIR SLOWLY
AND GENTLY!

## Art Process
1. Fill the grocery trays halfway to the top with water.
2. Gently drop a small amount of waterproof ink onto the surface of the water. Add drops of additional colors.
3. Stir the ink slowly and carefully over the water using a plastic spoon. (The ink will swirl and float, forming beautiful patterns.)
4. Place the blotting paper on top of the floating colors for about thirty seconds.
5. Quickly lift the paper, turn it over, and hold it flat to stop the colors from running.
6. Allow the colored paper to dry on a flat, covered surface. This project can take several days to dry.

## Variation
- This project is very pretty to watch using a clear, glass bowl with a piece of plain white paper beneath it. Skip the paper-printing step and just enjoy watching the colors swirl and mix in the bowl.

## Hints
- Use small squares of paper to make this project easier to control.
- Supervision is necessary when working with waterproof ink.

QUICKLY
LAY THE PAPER
FLAT AND FACE UP!

# Batik Eggs

## Materials

scissors
crepe paper, several
   colors
bowls
hot water
tweezers
measuring spoons

white vinegar
candle
matches
hard-boiled eggs
paper towels
cookie tray
oven
egg carton or aluminum
   foil

## Art Process

1. Cut strips of crepe paper about ½" (1 cm) wide. Place each color in a separate bowl.
2. Pour hot water over the crepe paper to release the dye (supervise closely). Use tweezers or your fingers to remove the paper from the water.
3. Add 1 tablespoon (15 ml) white vinegar to each bowl and let the mixture cool.
4. Light the candle (adult only) and drip candle wax onto the eggs. The waxed parts of the egg will remain uncolored. This step should be closely supervised.
5. Decorate the eggs using several applications of wax and dye. Begin the process by dipping the egg in the lightest color of dye. Dry the egg with a paper towel.
6. Drip more candle wax on the parts of the egg that you want to remain light-colored. Dip the egg into the next darker shade of dye, then dry it with a paper towel.
7. Cover a cookie tray with paper towels.
8. To remove the wax, place the eggs on the cookie tray and place it in a very warm oven. After the wax has melted (about 2 minutes), wipe the eggs with a paper towel.
9. Allow the eggs to cool in an egg carton or on a piece of wrinkled aluminum foil.

*AFTER THE WAX REMOVAL!*

## Hints

- This is a one-on-one project. The adult will likely do most of the work, but encourage the child do as much as possible.
- Empty fresh eggs by poking a pinhole in both ends of it and blowing out the contents with a hefty puff of air. The empty egg will be fragile and light, but it will keep indefinitely.

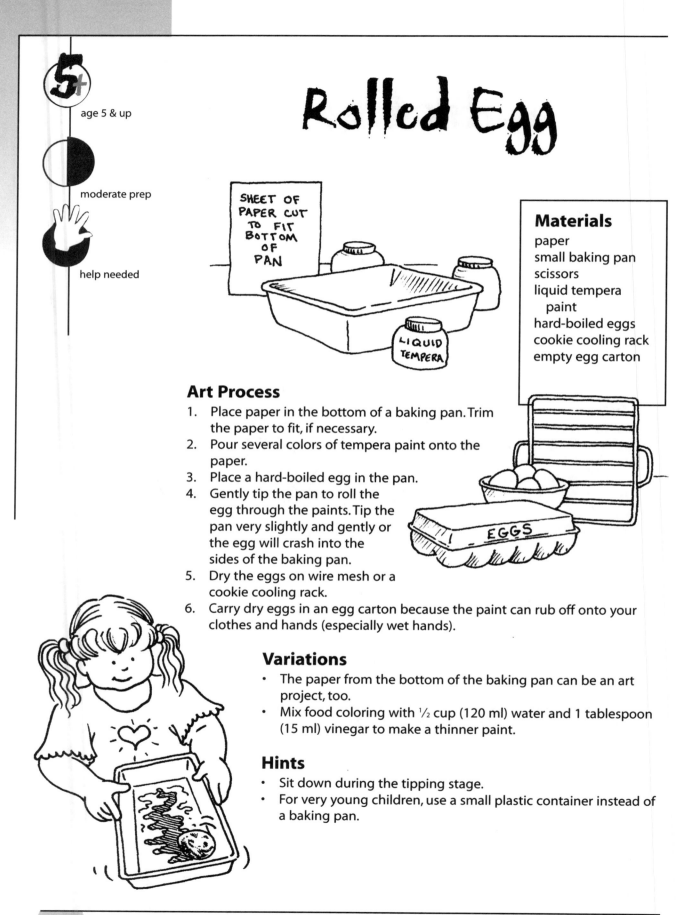

age 5 & up

moderate prep

help needed

# Rolled Egg

SHEET OF PAPER CUT TO FIT BOTTOM OF PAN

LIQUID TEMPERA

### Materials
paper
small baking pan
scissors
liquid tempera
   paint
hard-boiled eggs
cookie cooling rack
empty egg carton

EGGS

## Art Process

1. Place paper in the bottom of a baking pan. Trim the paper to fit, if necessary.
2. Pour several colors of tempera paint onto the paper.
3. Place a hard-boiled egg in the pan.
4. Gently tip the pan to roll the egg through the paints. Tip the pan very slightly and gently or the egg will crash into the sides of the baking pan.
5. Dry the eggs on wire mesh or a cookie cooling rack.
6. Carry dry eggs in an egg carton because the paint can rub off onto your clothes and hands (especially wet hands).

## Variations

- The paper from the bottom of the baking pan can be an art project, too.
- Mix food coloring with ½ cup (120 ml) water and 1 tablespoon (15 ml) vinegar to make a thinner paint.

## Hints

- Sit down during the tipping stage.
- For very young children, use a small plastic container instead of a baking pan.

# Onion Skin Egg

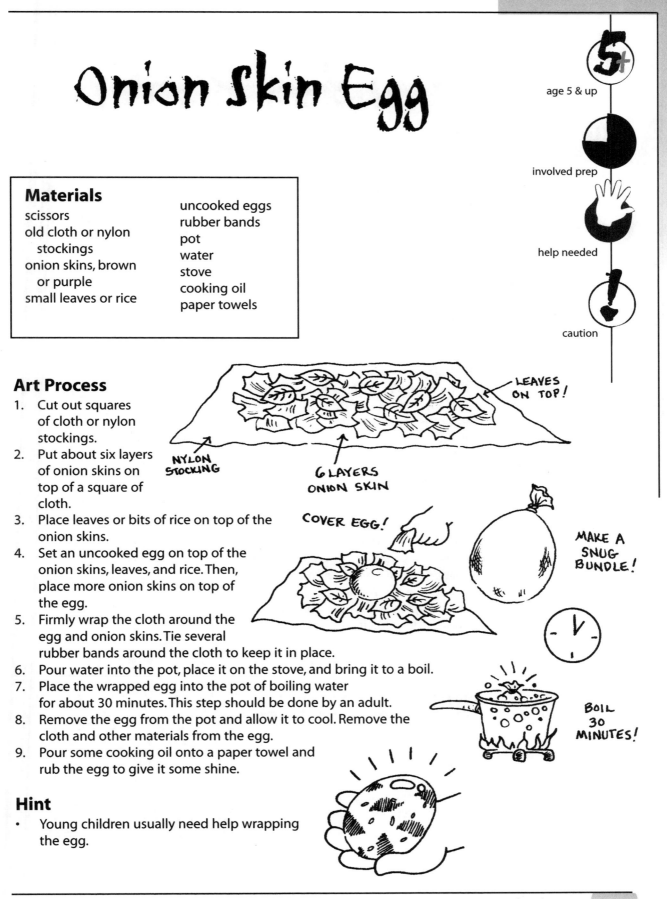

age 5 & up

involved prep

help needed

caution

## Materials

scissors
old cloth or nylon
  stockings
onion skins, brown
  or purple
small leaves or rice

uncooked eggs
rubber bands
pot
water
stove
cooking oil
paper towels

## Art Process

1. Cut out squares of cloth or nylon stockings.
2. Put about six layers of onion skins on top of a square of cloth.
3. Place leaves or bits of rice on top of the onion skins.
4. Set an uncooked egg on top of the onion skins, leaves, and rice. Then, place more onion skins on top of the egg.
5. Firmly wrap the cloth around the egg and onion skins. Tie several rubber bands around the cloth to keep it in place.
6. Pour water into the pot, place it on the stove, and bring it to a boil.
7. Place the wrapped egg into the pot of boiling water for about 30 minutes. This step should be done by an adult.
8. Remove the egg from the pot and allow it to cool. Remove the cloth and other materials from the egg.
9. Pour some cooking oil onto a paper towel and rub the egg to give it some shine.

LEAVES ON TOP!

NYLON STOCKING

6 LAYERS ONION SKIN

COVER EGG!

MAKE A SNUG BUNDLE!

BOIL 30 MINUTES!

## Hint

- Young children usually need help wrapping the egg.

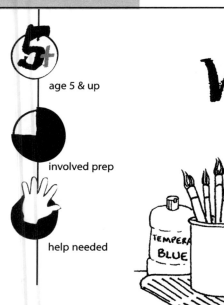

# Window Painting

**age 5 & up**

**involved prep**

**help needed**

## Materials

newspaper
tape
liquid tempera
   paint
containers
paintbrushes
sponge and soapy
   water

## Art Process

1. Tape newspaper to the bottom edges of the windows to protect the floor and window ledges.
2. Pour the tempera paint into containers.
3. Paint designs on the inside of the window. This will prevent rain from washing them off.
4. Wash off the design with a sponge and soapy water.

## Variations

- Paint holiday scenes or use holiday colors to paint designs.
- Cover the window with a large sheet of cellophane and paint on that instead of directly on the window.
- Try using white shoe polish in an applicator bottle instead of tempera paint.

## Hints

- You can leave the design on the windows for days or weeks. However, the longer you leave the paint on the window, the harder it will be to remove.
- To make removal easier, mix the powdered tempera paint with liquid dishwashing soap and water or use white shoe polish.

# Index

Swinging Paint, 43
Tissue Stain, 30
Twist and Shout, 28
Vegetable Dye, 13
Watercolor Paint, 11
Window Painting, 58

# Materials Index

**50 great ways to explore and create with paper, feathers, buttons, and other easy-to-find materials!**

# Preschool Art
# Collage and Paper
*MaryAnn F. Kohl*

Encourage children to experience the joy of exploration and discovery with this new series by MaryAnn F. Kohl. Excerpted from the national best-sellers **Preschool Art** and **MathArts,** this book emphasizes the process of art, not the product. **Preschool Art: Collage and Paper** gives you 50 great ways to create with paper, feathers, buttons, and other easy-to-find materials. Make art fun and accessible to children of all ages with these creative, easy-to-do activities!

## ISBN 0-87659-252-3 / Gryphon House / 15726 / $7.95

Available at your favorite bookstore, school supply store, or order from Gyphon House at 800.638.0928 or www.gryphonhouse.com.

50 great ways to explore and create with playdough, tissue mâché, yeast dough, peanut butter dough, and more!

# Clay and Dough

## *MaryAnn F. Kohl*

Encourage children to experience the joy of exploration and discovery with this new series by award-winning author MaryAnn F. Kohl. Excerpted from the national best-seller **Preschool Art,** each book in the series emphasizes the process of art, not the product. **Preschool Art: Clay & Dough** gives you 50 great ways to create with playdough, tissue mâché, yeast dough, peanut butter dough, and more. Make art fun and accessible to children of all ages with these creative, easy-to-do activities!

**ISBN 0-87659-250-7 / Gryphon House / 16928 / $7.95**

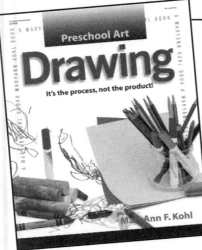

50 great ways to explore and create with chalk, crayons, stencils, textures, and more!

# Drawing
## *MaryAnn F. Kohl*

Encourage children to experience the joy of exploration and discovery with this new series by award-winning author MaryAnn F. Kohl. Excerpted from the national best-seller **Preschool Art,** each book in this new series emphasizes the process of art, not the product. **Preschool Art: Drawing** gives you 50 great ways to create with chalk, crayons, stencils, textures, and more! Make art fun and accessible for children of all ages with these creative, easy-to-do activities.

**ISBN 0-87659-223-X / Gryphon House / 19658 / $7.95**

Available at your favorite bookstore, school supply store, or order from Gyphon House at 800.638.0928 or www.gryphonhouse.com.